Horses In Boiling Blood

Apollinaire
MacSweeney

a collaboration
a celebration

Thanks are due to Lilian McSweeney, Desmond Graham, Helen Arkwright and Jackie Litherland, for their help in the preparation of this edition. Publication was made possible by a generous grant from the Arts Council of England.

'Secret Poem Number Nine' (1997 version) originally appeared in *Fire*, 14 magazine in the Barry MacSweeney Tribute section, May 2001, edited by Jeremy Hilton. 'Fancy Nancy' originally appeared in *Sand*, Issue One, 2003, edited by Kevin Cadwallender.

Typeset in Baskerville by Sam Ladkin
Cover image by Barry MacSweeney
Published by Equipage
c/o Rod Mengham
Jesus College
Cambridge
CB5 8BL

ISBN 1 900968 76 2

ARTS COUNCIL ENGLAND

Horses In Boiling Blood

MacSweeney

Contents

War Roses

poem LXXVI – Poems à Lou, Apollinaire p230

Such amazing fireworks light over steel
Total forked lightning beautiful and true
Madfire murderers Madmen flamebearers
Smiling with courage you periscope the enemy

Two Himalayan roses brilliantly exploding
Expanding like breasts their very best bra-hooks
Stretching out bedroom-darkened fingertips
They must love to tell the German sky They're dead now

A poet inside Kielder Forest
Stands flinty and aloof from the pain
His French Army issue revolver on safety
Some roses of this war die in complete silence

Roses abandoned dying and dying: comrades
He will strap his gob upon the cool park fountain
Beside the runback path through the escape trees
I walk there every night – fast – like Oscar Wilde

The roses – my men – bleed like subjects from the rimdom
of the Marquis de Sade – and suddenly his head bends over –
a beautiful red rose reduced and reduced by Bosche brutality
Spreadeagled like your bedroom-lit softly curved haunch-hips

The air is crammed with completely mad spirits
Sieved through the light of newly-discovered stars
Howitzers weep above us in their sudden flight
Death, shattered petals, loving death to France's finest

*

Every single promise of love is well below you
And who will put your signature on the world as a poet
O rose forever fresh despite bombardments O ready rose
Instead of beauty I offer disgusting perfume of death and blood

You flowers who will not give up your medals when surrendering
O permanent combat soldiers the dawn gusts have mistreated
you
Flowers soldiers combat conscripts filled with hope of victory
They are wrapped up linament thank Christ no more bleeding

They cry as I approach them
I am only trepanned and have lost no limbs
The Pearlmoon is so tender
We flow backwards into our tidal gutterage & filth

It is as fatal as a great Northumbrian piper who will not listen

I balance my future air on the crystal of clouds
My badness at once will vanish from me despite this terrible war

And clouds will now very soon claim and clam down upon us
dark & unforgiving   forever

July 1998

Troubled Are These Times

Cushy days have gone forever
    from marigold beds   to a land called Hell
My ring blue but the mind is oppressed and black
    Cushy days heaven on earth crushed and gone
Cowboy bootlace ties snapped and hoyed
    Mist around the Tour Eiffel has turned to fog
I am no longer up to thighs in trench-water
    I am up to my Adam's Apple in the dreaded gargle
O Esmerelda   Drive that taxi drive that cab
    Keep this broken poet & brother off the cold cold slab
We want a future   We want to see the herbs
    Re-seed for at least eight million years
It is almost winter and we want to see
    Northumbrian snow sleeving the beautiful boughs
It will be like wedding dresses right through the forest
    Words that spring to mind will be **bridal** and **virgin**
And the only **darkness** will be layered like silk
    On the little wings of the snow bunting not yet left
The Kielder Ride potholed in the way we love
    Paris only two train trips away   One under the sea
6:10am exactly but darke this September dawn
    Darke and darke from one soul to another
Fame will come upon us but for most different reasons
    We shall be found in the night stretched and strung
Unless protected against the endless harm of the world
    Harmlessness such a precious condition these days
Rage will seek and find its squadrons of permanent ire
    And there will be nothing left but night night night
And within the night there will be night night night
    The heartbroken however will seek & find their true station
Esmerelda drive that yellow taxi through the pouring rain
    There is no tomorrow and the snow bunting has flown
There is no tomorrow and all swannes have deserted the Elvet
    There is no outlook and the dashing sky-high swifts
Have abandoned the large and lowering cloud formations
    Darling o Darling there is no tomorrow only coffins
It used to be pelting rain but now it is tears pouring down
    There is dawn sunshine dearest but heart cleavage is royal
And at the bitter corrosive forefront of all of our sad duration
    Darling our axles poles rods shafts spindles
Our chassis
Is broken destitute and completely penniless
these awful days
    I am the original Elvet swanne with blanch wings
I swanned alone in the wreckage of riverweeds waiting for Thee
    All I ate was a destitute menu of brook sludge
Waiting to twin and twine my snowy nuzzle and hugneck

The world gonne mad Mrs Goebells poisons her six children
They belong to Hitler and so they must die
No amount of sky as paper No amount of clouds No amount
of sea as ink can spell out the terrible awesome tragedy
It's the thinness of the limbs and skulls and the six-pointed starre
Which tears apart and breaks your so-called civilized hearte
May the eighth May the eighth May the eighth May the eighth
Returning to the walking position if possible the children
Experimented upon with injections by Dr Mengele & amputations

I have exchanged my beloved stone walls for sinks and sickness
For the longing lutes of sadness which drive mad my brain
All the crosses on the graves demand reason for conflict
And the ire will ascend like fire and torch our minds
It will scorch us for not importing the guillotine
and not executing enough members of the royalty

Treachery and dumb appointments stalk the mad earthe
We try and avoid their cunning devious shadows
So they do not fall upon our Cuban-heeled biker boots
And sully our already badly-riddled heartes & soules

A singular circlet of amateur arrangements has harassed
My neck all day worse than the German gunnes
This was a peak of underachievement at its berry vest
It is an icon of Gerry the Bosche at his very best

There is that moment when the gunnes start and you think
I should have written another postcard to Jacqueline
And several other treasured people you love admire and need
To make sure the corpse gets home and is destroyed with dignity

As a mark of respect
We are closing France
My wonderful France
We are shutting it down
It isn't far in the Larousse

From Guillaume
To Guillotine

Four million will stand in the trenches and watch the one coffin
There will be postcards from loved ones tomorrow and the cafés
Will he locked and bolted against the invasion of terrible death
We have received all betrayals now and I want to hear from Pablo

I want to kiss the black saddle & the bicycle steel horns of the bull
There are thousands of Joan Miro sunnes and they Will rise again
But there are no postcards from Dusty They are suspended
Because of the great beauty of the nation I respect grieve for & love

O Paris my dearest when will I see Thee again
    My Milky Way my cobblestones My brilliant cafés
I will not even catch the Metro from Gare de Lyon
    I will walk up the Rue St Denis to the Agile Rabbit

Mmm Who are you in the white silk stockings Ah Madeleine
    When a German Howitzer shell crashes into your face
Just before your head comes off Your inner tongue
Spouts it out: To whom shall your officers send the telegrams

I stand here thigh-high in muddy water blitzed by shelles
& quite frankly I don't care who are the lieutenants of the future
And you talk to me about refutation and difficult positions
    Nor will I talk about it Leave I'm sending shells which explode

Green leaves are turning to brown especially in the crater holes
    Where with the cordite upon them they have been awarded
No natural end to their lives on the tips of the trees
    They are like my comrades Burned to eternal life i.e. Death

Their boots are now a funny shape lying in the mudde
        And their heads even stranger no eyes and noses
I saw one of my sergeants with seven fingers
    When I had coffee with him this morning he had ten
And two thumbs One of which he used to cock a rifle

To split the hearts and skulls of those grey-suited primitives
who are trying to rape and overtake my gorgeous republic
They will not they will not those from the land of Bavarian cakes
I am from the republic of croissants and we shall repel them

O dear Napoleon you kissed the big flag and just like Thee
    I am France and France is me
Catching my left index finger pushing through the mud
    A broken-down gun-carriage I could barely write this poem

But what do you expect the waves were like those at Bordeaux
        And on the salt marshes and in Marseilles
When the tide comes in with the sardine fishing-boats
    I long for them and my heart is like an unplucked harpe

My tongue has not yet flicked along the holes of a harmonica
    I don't want gunnes I want Bob Dylan and Emmylou Harris
I want time to write a poem swifter than a snipe drumming
    Even the telephone here in the trench is not as sweet
as the cry of my beloved peewit as it skims the upland earthe

The radio telephone is monstrous and not bird beautiful
    Its messages when we lift the receiver suggest we may die today
It freezes your eyes and makes your heart so cold
    You dream of the young lass in the cous-cous café in Berbes

And you swaggered in   In your new motorbike jacket
                And the biker's obligatory white silk scarf
But she drew her burnt gold curtains against your fantastic
            Revving and against your fierce glare of pure magnetism

Yet I know here that we shall begin again in times of freedom
            When war has stopped its terrible intervention
And your little pair of dollypops high-heels are by the window
    Now we rue the very streets but soon we will be liberated

The diamond and other gem starres shine in the heavens
    Despite all the bullets which whizz above our heads
Mars ascends so scarlet shaming the other planets for brightness
    Except the moon which I singularly compare to Paris

It is a tangerine in a flood of aubergines
It is the light of my life
It is a candle lit when the darkest hour has come
It is
The truth

Inspired by Guillaume Apollinaire
Septre 6e 97

Miss The Mississippi and Thee

For Jimmie Rodgers and Iris DeMent

The world is completely drear without you and I am a lost planet
    swinging through the night in a universe of stupid pleasure
There is nothing left hanging onto the once-full hamshank
    It is but a bone packed with soft marrow fit only for dogs

There is a dawdling hand I remember hanging onto mine
    There is a pair of lips used to sipping tea speaking at dawn
And I used to speak too at the nether end of the double bed barefooted
    of the Gnosiennes and Erik's bicycle rides before this war

Overwhelmed with whitecaps of love
    Plaited and twined as the finest sailor's lanyard
        Naked and besilken and plaited and twined

There is a sunne in the sky but all I can see is darkness of the hearte
    It is trench-hot I am in shorts crematorium black to engage in death
I imagine all the angels which you sent me and I gaze at them for wings
    To lift me from the very torment which drives me to the earthe
Into the eternal bar-room of tomorrow and even to the Quick Rabbit

It is not solace it is not solace it is plague and spite inside your face
    I've washed and then dried my hair but it is absolutely no use
Without you I am only half a human being and I cannot walk anywhere
    I used to be a poetic cyborg complete with dapper bowler hat

but now I'm a stricken bombzombie in steel helmet bayonet quite fixed
    modern engineering gave us the Tower and the new powers to kill
I am in smithereens in tatters torn to shreds by your love withdrawal
    By your complete refusal to negotiate all and everything

As if suddenly I had become the Balkans instead of a strolling poet
    enjoying one more sunrise by Sonia Delaunay
No I have made my necessary pact with midnight of the mind
    And there will never be any repair truck called up available

The hopeless quartermasters far too busy playing cards and hoarding cigars
    There are no spanners or wrenches only those inside the soule
Unless once again we are twinned and twined like common white swannes
    Grenades everywhere not just beyond the sandbags soaked in blood

There is a maniac on the downhill slope called Gwillam Mad MacSweeney
    A corpse-crammed crevice has his name upon it writ large in snowe
At least one Bosch would like to deliver his calling card from Dresden
    So I lie flat wishing we were knitted together my oyster shell

Or so you said and then unravelled the very sleeves which held us close
Everything broken gone and smashed to the boiling ground
We have gonne the way of three o'clock in the afternoone The way of the bull
We have gone all the way of the sword to the strong hearte we have
Gone

We have gone to the horseman to the picador
We have gone to the caped one in the ring of hot sande

A telegraph arrived from the one-handed operator of Morse
ELVIS DIES AT 42 **This is a world of hot strange wands & moves**
One day we take a trench through the wire and the next we are without it
Come what may no matter the moon no matter the Mons moon

We are in the absolute lampblack of lovelessness and there is no return
France may fall before the fangs of the German temperament
We have already raised a cowardly white flag above our love
Goodbye sweetest darling I know it is Forever Your vow deserted now

Août 1997/Mars 98
after Apollinaire

Feast of Fashion Burning Down: ZonE

Man among heart-thieves, endless disputes
man alone with 40,000 others
in a starre-system of their own
    where the aeroplanes go
we flew apart at the end of the old world
we flew together and then apart in a feast of moons and heifers
oddly-coutured harlequins beneath a high harvest
when you are dreaming of Pearl
and it is too long drinking & dreaming
newspapers every day and their manifold police stories

shock

horror

Probe

meanwhile the Germans are bombing us as if no tomorrow – which there isn't
the new cars are invading the streets of Paris   forgive our gaz
On the other hand, don't We are modernists
I am spit on the pavement

I have your tears and tears on the telephone
I saw this morning a beautiful street whose name I don't remember
it was Northumberland Street, Newcastle-upon-Tyne
A city I have never been to and do not remember

I went once to Hexham and stamped my little feet
They looked at me sideways
I stood at the war memorial
not knowing that my dad had fought in the trenches
before he left us and never spent any time teaching me the ABC
like you did

And he never loved you as you should have been loved as I loved you
As I plucked
                                        a marigold

before you said Mayakovsky
Esenin
and I
bloody boy Chatterton Shelley Shakespeare and Blake

WHAT WAS THAT **FIRST** WORD

R

        a
i
n

it was filled with women of unusual hue and fantastic attraction
every day that passes a siren goes   not any more! Swans dead

Everything clamours: the big signs, the big men, the darling secretaries
all the way from Monday to Saturday – and now, of course, Sunday!
This what I said to the day: you fuck, you fuck, [Pacino] you German
aeroplanes. But how the skies are so exquisitely gorgeous and filled with
peachen light.

The entire universe is jacks and planes and locks and doors
and abstract ideas in which there will be plenty of time to remember.

Adios America apparently so the voyages in my head are just too far

The voyages of the clouds are such beauty I never want to be attacked in the
mud. The aeroplanes can hammer us but we will not die.

I am a poet and a fighter not a Pope

                                        you don't know the intricacies and
lunacies of the cathedrals and love

here is the young street
the one of blue and white
it's nine o'clock the petrol has gone from the tanks
and now you're asleep with someone else
while we die in the trenches

All the flies fly by

and the tremendous resurgence of the troops has ended
thank goodness

You pray all of the night in the wings and shadows of the
Dartington college in Devon with the American deconstruction mistress
to where you have not visited and sniffed cocaine

There is an amethyst profundity in the whole of the universe
which will never turn to the eternal glory of the Jesus Christ Almighty
ever
We always aim towards the eternal beautiful
it is the beautiful blue and dark blue lilies
which we used to cultivate

I have a million reasons for bringing them to you, savage, every one,
a man alone, without future, it is nothing and I have nothing to lose

They are the most glorious and magnificent lilies we have ever grown
It's the torch in the red hair that will not be extinguished by the wild
wind
Never turn to the flamboyant glory of Jesus
That's the pale boy and painfully distressed mother
Forever it will be a fully-flushed tree beneath my praying palms
I am nowhere but in a trench miles away from Grey's Monument
That's the double gallows of honour and eternity

It's the starre of six branches of the night attack

It's the so-called God who dies on Monday and rises again on Saturday
It's Jesus the most sanctimonious man on TV and
It's not his fault
He's wearing a beard but he's not called Jesus he's called JeremyBeadle

Situated at Grey's Monument between Northumberland Street and the
children of the next universe
as in verse
It's Jesus who soars to the heavens higher than the aviators
He prevents everyone getting to the heights and sitting beside him

It's called death in the trenches beneath the aeroplanes
Pupilchild Jesus Christ Almighty of the eye on the world
the Pharisees and Germans came they were not even Nazis by then
there were no flashes no lightning strikes no Vingtième pupille
des siècles il sait y faire

It will all change when the bird dies and flows upwards towards Jesus
into the beautiful air

The demons in the rising gaping caverns know what to do
Elbow don't start rattling those bones around!
The demons raise your head above the parapet and then you
become a blonde with a head ready to be popped off by a German

The shadows say you are Judas and imitating Simon of the Desert
They chase you and try and catch after you in the street calling you a
thief: You fool! They say HE's The Thief! Icarus Enoch of
Birmingham Ely of Dublin Bobby Sands you madman Apollinaire

I only wanted to get up to urinate and say against the stark dawn light:
the fist comes out of the web of clothing like a leg of lamb

But it has no rosemary

Big poet man in the first-ever aeroplane – don't you deny me! I can see
you from here in les tranches
St Exupery, climb down!
Those prayers which arrive eternally upwards towards the host

Freakjob, handjob, kissjob, explosivemind subject,

The ibis on fire the crags of the maribou crane

Zero human, nowhere person, lost in the rain in New York
I do not want to keep a straight face You're a T-shirt
you're a gunne a fathom job so long helicopter pilotesse
you're a helicopter gunship you're a fucking rave maniac

It's the wrong time the incorrect place the inconvenient moment
That's the zebra hour it's the place of the ibis the squarm of the stalk
It's the palace, the Utopia, Zion, the home of God, the quack of the duckwalk

Savage childe, remember your endlessly mindless place

Senior matrons boss me and don't believe me that I was in an endless
aerodrome I was I was A French poet killed in World War One
I wore a Bowler Hat what will you do Give Me A medal?
dorsiflexion comes upon us we arrive at the badly moment time

bonetime is a thing of the living world and not for thee
and hopefully not for me here in the grave trenches I wish

gapeful we stretch into the daylight trying our best to believe
and seeking breakfasts we search and search looking for succulence

O golden eagle

Let me wear my white stockings and my high-heeled high-strapped
cobbledehoys and sit upon you until we both come and let the Germans
die

When I'm worn out myself I will tear the Zeppelins from the sky
unroll my stockings and curl my feet against yours like gondolas

THE SKY IS EMPTIED now OF MILLIONS OF SWALLOWS

the angels flit about authorized by the happy flitter

the eagle from the air disturbs the hiboux

then is the immaculate voice of the spirit of columbine

and the swerving sky-ridden peacocks brought in the encyclopedia bought by
Susan

The next minute you're a pile of passionate ashes

Here we are in the perilous straits and confines
The sirens of death are appealing to the ends of the earth
The calls of the guns are arriving three by three
They are such friendly and familiar violent machines

Now you walk in Paris completely alone through the throng
The busflocks lowing in the avenues and boulevards rolling by

The phoenix butcher will be reborn again
the very moment that you are reduced to filth and furnace-endings
thinking you'll never live
You Lazarus driven insane by sunlight you bastard
You German twats
You men with machine-guns
You murderers of the French
You stupid invaders

Corstopitum cor petal
the Romans have gone and Aislinn
to London and Geneva
I am bereft of sense
but I can reach her on the mobile

087 564248

don't torment yourself with the open address book to Dublin

you'll fall in the Forty Foot you'll jump in the Murphy's before the

Germans come
You'll die of a bombed out bowler hat
You'll fleece yourself you'll
you'll do that you'll
There is no shameful disease there is no question there is Nothing
There is Zone Zero
There are only big guns   It is a complete nightmare   A voice in the
darkness Forgive me Lord I am in a trench   It is Nothing

It is only with my Strength and everyone else's
that we save the world from the Great Beast

May light dying it is forever daylight except at night

Farewell
The sun is chopped off by its neck
The sun is strangled
And so are my comrades

Autumn 1997
Inspired by Apollinaire
from ***ZONE***

Terrible changes

A woman bleats & cries in the night She has lost her bloke
Howay pet O howay our lass
Just because you've lost your fella The lads are marching back from hospital towards the Germans
O howay honey I'll take you doon the Bigg Market
Where your clip-clops and groovy stockings

I'll take you out in white courts from Next doon the Toon
First Bourgognes Then The Duke We'll stagger down Dean Street
and celebrate our great victory of love over darkness
O Killhope Wheel by the recovery farmhouse where the medics wait for work
flaying the untickled brown trout from the burn
There's nowt we can do about it flower The wheel must crush lead

Howay man pet we'll go to the Fujiyama for sushi and beef
Come on honeybunch I'll buy you a new bra in Fenwick's
I'll buy it while you drift elegantly to the food department to buy the Napoli Salami
The Fenwick's deli is the best in town
Our trenches were lit up by the brightness of shells destroying real men
Can you imagine only one arm at the age of 24

Hey Pizzaland! Here we go!
I've seen the shells open the skie like petals and blow legs off
Petlamb divvent worry It's the Quayside for us
Tuxedo Royale

You fear everything has altered
In my heart
But nowt has
I'm your crazed lover
EVERYTHING
My love is saved forever
Turks Head Here We Come!!

after Apollinaire
Septre 97 Just before the Hellhound Trail Tour

21

Sonnet written on February 8 1915

Monday Feb 8 my petlamb
My dollbird's gone
Troubled heart scrammed
Calvados for everyone

Truly we are servants of Austria
(Spuds in pigfat)
Army suffering cash gonorrhoea
I am in the madness van

Hope lives like man and wife with fear
Death too like that
I salute France sweet service my dear

Poet gunner
My soul bounds to your ordered bedroom
So long stunner

***

March 18 1998
After Apollinaire's XXI Poèmes à Lou
[Shadow Love]

Six

Canteen Gauloises smoke broody nightmarsh fugfog
Wise voices afraid voices Jesus thornblood wine everywhere
I join the smoke again but this time with comrades & fire up a pipe
Tomorrow we all shave again for the sweetfields & meadows of war
They will try and sleep while it pluts under argent-buckled Betelgeuse
They'll hoy themselves like me into a pillion point of gun triumphs
Just like me we'll all obey the same frontline commandments
Their ears are open acute to all the brilltop bugle calls from behind
They will die next to me and perhaps I will die next to them
They will suffer in snow and bleed under sunshine right with me
They will understand and obey with me the leisure of man
They look at the Bossbabes heading from Haymarket to Monument
They want them all of them but my love stakes higher ground
She is warrior queen of my heart my senses and my modernist mind
Who is my Cowshill my Lanehead my upland shaking holes all hopes
To me kisspout pushlip loving soldier of my creamy luscious France

Mars 17e 98
after Apollinaire's VI Poèmes à Lou
[Shadow Love]

Ode To Snowe

after Apollinaire's L'avenir

I cannot wait for the froste to come
It will harden the sprouts and cool my ardent heart
But like the vegetables it will harden my sapper's sap
And make my heart truer to you than it has Ever been

Roll the bales of hay for winter
The farms will need them when war is done
Write your letters to dear ones
And stand to attention when told to

Let us smoke a pipe at nightfall
And dream of recovering love
The lieutenants are all around us
But enjoy the trench dogroses

The torrent of shells upon us never fails
The sky still gold And the hay good for the cannon horses
Just look at the bee
And don't think of the future

Look at our hands firing the artillery
They are as white as snow with the cold and rain
The dogroses running wild and the bee
And the future   I shrug   is also vicious violent and untamed

Août 97

Victory Over Darkness & The Sunne

after Apollinaire
and in memory of Tatlin Esenin
Mayakovsky and Malevich

Grouse bark in the heatherholes and the whitebeams
play musick like Corelli and Handel by the East Allen River
Their leaves sound in the night like the pleas of poor seamen
On the Herald of Free Enterprise upon its stricken side

Its hull balances swivelled into the sea and turned like Icarus
Turning from a god of travel to nothing more than a midge
The puddles reflect us as we walk and walk towards death

We smile a lot however drunk on the finest Bordeaux and Chianti

My diamond shining heart which will speak and speak forever
You're three hundred miles away now and I miss you and miss you
My lamps around the little house and my pierced helmet

Just look at the beautiful stone-cutting in Dean Street and Grainger
Street not to mention St Cloud and Sacre Coeur
The days were pure as beryl gems

The whole war from the trenches was like a firework display
The shells hung in the air like roses and other flowers
Fetching blood and light and other stranger beings

You became scared of the sky
like a bout of unstoppable hiccups

You thought at night about the difficulties
Because our success depended on fellow people being dumb and stupid
Officers for example
There is a new language to learn at war
Youngsters have to be prepared to die at will

When the academics stay at home like 1968 and have nowt to say
When their minting of coinage is stooped in a university study

The language needed a blood transfusion and was near death
It lacked life and was beaten to fear and death by several poets
They did not do any good to poetry and were not there when it mattered

Did you notice how they weren't on the ferry to Paris in 1968?
They're just a bunch of silent film starres

But if we work tough enough
the language will be kept alive
And the mutants & enemies will be driven down

We want new sounds not neat Faber and Faber
We want new sounds no Simon Armitage
with hands in the pockets of his suit in Paris
half a pound of badly-fried chips on each shoulder

I say: Fight the language which is nailed and then driven down!
To let it go is a sign of complete lack of civilization
But reclaiming it   my dearest poets
is a tremendous prize

Our Katie gives me two daisies picked from Whitbeck Road
making more noise of the heart than what we say
Saying she loves me   and I kiss her lip better   Twice
Farewell memories of the past   Pure nostalgia
Nobody likes the nomadic nature of love
When you hope for new & beautiful women to come into your life
O my dear darling dollbird hurry home
As soon as the Great North Eastern Railway will bring thee
And
Look at the way I look at you with a clearer eye

These hopeless railway companies are making me yodel with sadness
They are ridiculous but trains are always beautiful
In the pouring rain on Platform 2 the 2 lights of the 225 shine in the mist
Reminding me of the fantastic shine of your grin in the rain
I bow over like a wedding ceremony to kiss you And your freshly-trimmed
hair   You great beauty
And I am miserable that we aren't together even though like Elvis sang
I wear your lapis and silver ring
Our laughter even when we talk on the telephone spreads like butter

All around the house and the very world

Let's speak with our hands and clap them together in a high-five
Let's strike them like a gypsy tambourine Wild and famous
O you wildwind words
She walks through the berried rowan
Love and no love walk around crying out their eyes
I am the sky over Greys Monument
I am the sky beyond the Haymarket and beyond that

Listen to the roaring tide at Craster and the Farnes

Listen to the moaning tide faraway at Dunbar singular and lonely
My faithful voice in the darkness of Denton Burn
You think you are the last clear voice on earthe
The tidal causeway at Lindisfarne can be as untrue as you
Just as Basil taught me all of those years ago

And he said if you don't publish correctly the tidal charts
Seamen from Valparaiso and Houston will end up on the Black Middens
dead on the rocks

Their cries echoing under the tidal sweep like the organs
of St Nicholas and St Mary's in the hearte of the city
And like St Denise in the outskirts of beloved Paris
And when the sun rises from the fjords' darkness
will only be in their death if you do not correct your tidal charts
Accuracy is all he said and also compression of language

Words are all we cannot live without   They tremble in the night
You should say to your hands please do not forget me
I love both of you at the typewriter and also at Persian prayer

What a relief it will be   a real Fenwick's window to hug you
You know   There will be many new things to do Now we're not at warre

O my tongue slurs but I wish to lap the shore of life
and sound like Kerouac's Big Sur
And from St Malo to Craster and Seahouses
I speak the beautiful language of the Northumbrian waves

Sometimes I convulse and fit and my hands sleep in the street
until children find me and call the paramedics

Yet my fingers like me are face down in the heart of the city
My eyelids broken and lips bleeding I stagger home Streets dead
Longing for the sharp winds of my homelands

As dead as the rail company which has cancelled all trains after 10.40pm
Look   Listen

Victory over all enemies is before us
Including addiction
Look towards the future
Look towards everything you can see
Or your dearest loved ones

And give your life a new name

Oui!

Alors finis
C'est tout
Août 24

In Charge Of The Lads

I'm gobsmacked by the arduous wonders of genocide   Hell in France
My mouth here at 5am is sweetness nevertheless and even seduction
And I yearn for Margharete My Margharete my Lou

The mouth angels I have are mutilating your beautiful hearte
The fellow comrades in my regiment are getting ready for the assault against the Germans
The prayers I carry in my mouth which I carry into battle say first your name and your beauty Jackie will be with me forever under the gunnes
Your soul shaking rattling and rolling like us under the heavens
And the wildness of the German artillery trembling and trembling
We exist to save the world from its suicidal madness and therefore
Our eyes are as bright as they ever could be with the mission ahead
My mouth is an army of contraries like William Blake's

Like a magician who turns and transforms the very earthe
The rockbands and the dawnchoruses of my mouth [when I have stopped practising my Elvis stance with bent knees]
Are bringing my love to Thee

And though the shells are crashing I can hear your voice from Pity Me

When I rise and see the snow-laden wilderness of Alston

I can't wait for the fight to begin

So we conquer and win

Août 97
After Apollinaire's
Chef de Section

The Heartbroken Starre

There is a woman who understands my trepanned head
She stands and gazes at Mars and never lets me down
All the reasons are where we live and in the sudden beautiful sky
Where the big man Burt Lancaster or Mary Magdalene strap on holsters

I'm not extracting the urine even though you're a Makem supporter
I believe in the starres just like Blake and that greatest man Percy Shelley
But the greatest sickness which feeds my never-ending rabies and delirium
Is that I know I will be upright on earthe and then go straight to HELL

Like the torn-up poems of my sevenyearoldhood committed by dad
And I mean committed   While the bodies of France lie around me
And heartflames stirre the very depths of France from St Malo to Florac
And like Ben's rocking guitar it fills the very air and shakes the fever pollen
Not just from the flowerfever
But also my hayfever nose

Août 97

Lost pity

Hadaway   Hadaway with you   my rainbow
Just go away and lose yourselves my gorgeous spectra
Your exit from my sight is utterly essential
In this time of shattered valleys and hills
all the way from Dirt Pot to the main street in Nenthead

St John's Chapel is but a lost horizon

And now the rainbow my belle rainbow is gone
But the iris we brushed against ourselves naked has not
And the curtains have not yet been opened
Take your place by the winds from the fjords and feel free
After a fulmar blown towards the hills by the storm on creaking wings

Août 97
after Apollinaire

Cornflower

Young poet Barry
only 20
Already you have witnessed the appalling world
What is your judgement on the adults who betrayed you

You   You
        faced
                death
                        on the   learned ways of cheating
                                beautiful
                                                Motor Guzzi
                                                                Californian
                                                                        drunk
                                                                                1,000 times
You told Elaine

    You were a brave nightrider

                And crashed
smashing yo   ur knees
On the A20   Then the M20 as if they named it after You
                handsome bridegroom
Filled with endless happiness
And covered in the blood of a wedding

                My heart a huge Soviet flag

                        Ray Davidson and Mark Hyatt had already died by their
own hands   Wilful and deranged
        Despite the efforts of me with Ray   I spat Ray   She isn't worth it
He would not take off his Mod glasses and would not listen at the Big
Lamp

and Jeremy and me on the nightride to Manchester
                One with chloroform and one with pothole pills
In that order

                At 5pm you rang and said goodbye   My bride
                And I drank myself to death   Twice   Three times   Four

    I learned nothing from my so-called betters
        But I am a sterner Miltonic man
                I stared death in the face
                        but not life
                O darling times in the various Kentucky and Tennessee
blue grasses
                        We're at the stupid red lights now

Août 97
After Apollinaire

Cold Mountain Ode

I am Cold Mountain and Wolf on the Treeline
I am fargone on a galleon and an oil-seeping tanker
I have travelled all of the way to the Orient and still never been there
There is no truth in Beauty Keats was error-ridden

Yet still I give it all the world's credence with a capital consonant
There are 365 days in one year and I have seen all of them 49 times
Why should I Be Lonely sings Aaron in one of Jimmie's best songs
I am Cold Mountain the wolfish monk who stalks the top of the lawrim

I speak to the wild geese in the garden and know them better than Thee
I lie flat on my stupid back and watch the Arctic terns and know them better
Than thee than thee than thee than thee than thee denier of my hearte
I travelled with Prynne through the Kielder Ride and we spoke

Of the abstract beauty of the planted larches and firs
And amazingly spotted in the pathway a snow bunting
And when we rode up to the Scot border Prynne said Wyoming
And for once in my life I knew it was absolutely veritable and true

And I knew that one day in the future with monk's paw I would write it down
The sleeve of the habit on the right arm would have to be retrieved
And that the eternal hood of the man in black would have to be demolished
And that the buttons would have to be sewn back onto your suits
Because you were never meant to be a Menonite or Amish but always a Mod
And black suits are in man skybluesocks and handmade Cheaneys or
Grensons   White socks are passé so very James Dean frownwise
And when the grain tumbles into the silos you will need a hat
Today midnight the first Harvest moone of the year bronze coin
And Guillaume drops in another postcard saying he'll be back
Despite the trepanning and his expected long stay in hospital
Before being transported with the rest of the lads back to shoot at Germans
O World your beauty is a crazed expression I see it every day but can't believe
Men with one hand and half an arm hauled back to the Front appalling
They should have been sent home to the vingtième arrondissement
The twentieth the only Communist one remaining in Paris and selling chard
They should have been delivered back to their homes near the Bastille
To the home of the tricolour and the settlements of the black flag
From the waisthigh water and the stars of the wilful shrapnel
Every man had a poem under his helmet and there was no tomorrow
Good Lord what IS going on in this place Bill Dead   Allen gone   Is Ed dead
I wake up at last and get the news It happens And I drink 230 pints of wine
And I see you and we agree some kind of arrangement which is right by me
And right by you and on your glasses go like a protection against Barglare
Split infinitives are a special portion of my nature just lately
Especially when berated at the crossroads between Ashleigh Road and The
Drive by your so-called mother and being branded evil in front of neighbours
At nine-thirty in the morning as if a complete criminal I am drunk but deny it
Not a criminal but a human being with every effort to shake off the chains

After Gwill and Snyder and unfinished – so far Août 9

Postcards
Waist high
In the Trenches
With My little pen
I don't Mind
I May be an Officer
In charge of Artillery
But Above All I am A Poet
Despite my Busted Head

Sam Arrives To Take Grandad for the Dawn Tickling

I always envied it and thought he was well handsome
My Grandad with his grey spike hair often touched with engine oil
Our Calvert past is so tremendously noble and on the edge of a cliffe

It wasn't magic you know us kids kneeled there trying to learn
We sat next to Grandad thinking the whole world was in his pockets
And it was   with lorry spanner and intricate penknives

Staggering back in the absolute night from the Allenheads Inn
With a stop-off at Sam's at Dirt Pot for a final gulp of Scotch whisky
And Annie and me slept up there and I made stew from lap of lamb
I let the fat settle on the surface and then skimmed it off to make it clear
so the carrots and mushrooms wouldn't be clouded much to her curly-haired
surprise and delight and then we twined our toe-boats and gondolas in the firelight

I look upon these times with the greatest affection
These times of trout tickling and learning how to shoot a gun
Are so old now at Sparty   they just fade away on the gentlest of breezes

But these were important times   Mysterious blazing and true

Août 1997
After Apollinaire

I'm Waiting Forever

for Willie Nelson

Darling I hang around with burning passion by the Himalayan roses
I make carrot coriander and lemon balm soup yet eat it alone

I long for the hair upon the **nape** of your neck and cannot find it
Alone in my double bed in the very dead of night A terrible business
I walked into the streets at seven minutes past three this morning
two glasses brimfilled with dry white wine
one each hand drank themboth upon the landscaped pitheap
spring merle madness

it was pourplutting with rain**Darling** I long to kiss your little toes
size three to four It drives me mad

Dearest petlamb I may beckon the wine from time to time but always I will

beckon Elvis The Killer Buddy & Cash and your eternal brilliant heart

Which **shines** like an unusual brigand trove in the Northumberland night
O jailer of my eyelids
Thresher of my pussycat lashes
Forgive me
Je suis crazed personne
Je suis madness Je suis Bigg Market
I have turned into a replica of Paul Gascoigne
My veins are thickened with Cotes du Rhone and my nails are longer than they
used to be The guitar leans unplayed

But still I love you up here in the great uplands of the north
From Alston to Garrigill to Nenthead all the way to Dirt Pot
to the beckbend at Cowshill Lane

While the beautiful river streams into the sea and eternity

Août 97/Mars 98
after Apollinaire

Horses Boiling In Blood
or The Fenwick's Third Floor Hair-do

It snows and it is the darkest of Novembers
O Marghareta I look forward to our lunchtime coffee in Blackfriars
When the whitebeams have been ragged to ribbons
By the German artillery

It is a tragedy for the whole of the world not just France
We watch and watch broken insomniacs in the snow
crashing down before the gunnes
Between the repeated oceans of iron Trees pitchnaked gantries in the dawn
Yet still my heart rises like a willow in spring forever in love with Sheila
Jacqueline
As if we were still at the Newburn Tidal Mark or Wylam
Railway Bridge   Where Malevich gripped our hearts and minds

You thought I was nothing but an apple tree bearing fruit
I'm not dearest I have the very blossoms of love

Between the darkest dusks and the snows of early November
from Nenthead to Dirt Pot and the tulip beds by Allenheads YMCA
Poppies and men are dead but the flowers *will* live again
The seeds will live in the earthe and will be revived unlike nurses and me
In the brains and business of the survivors & those who haven't been there
There is life after all but we may not see it Ever
Every day every day I write my log for love of Marghareta Margharissa
Snow plates the whitebeam leaves with beautiful flowers on the trees
And I lose my fleece as a ram at the loss of my horse brothers
That you didn't protect hauling the cannons
You dim-witted officers on the horizon behind the lines

I walked into the Barbes
for the best cous-cous in town

The magpies who had escaped the ordnance
came in black and white wave after wave
We couldn't believe it in the trenches with so many human beings dead

I have never seen so much forlorn hair
& so many fingernails which suddenly stopped growing
Thank you Germans

You carry away my very love of the world and everything
including   Marghareta   of the white pinafore

O Rose my jealousy is a stalking panther
and I walk through the dark forests of the night
with Othello who truly is my bother brother

and my socks a columbine blue
and red and orange with white stripes like a sudden star system
O Marghareta you're as bonny as any Bigg Market pizza
I love your pineapple and ham deep fried curves your stash

of utterly brilliant pepperoni over which I shall scoff until gone

Your eyes gazing at the Blackfriars pigeons and seeing the cockdove's
throat bobbing up and down here in the egg-gawping lunchtime

If I think at your Eveorange the wild roses flame away
like the foam at Sipton Shield and will not stop from flowing
If I think my hands are raw like Fenwick's best salami

Then for just a moment I think Jesus and Jerry Lee Lewis come down to save me
And rescue my language as a poet wild in the treeline

To change thee to change thee
I love Thee as a Swanne forever

Your face in the sunlight a bouquet of mixed flowers from Rushworth and Storey
by Gare du Nord
I couldn't see you today at Grey's Monument or the Haymarket
But you were at one of the Metro stations
You broke my heart you broke my little soldier's modernist heart
And I wake in the garden your garden of all overgrown twisted stems
It wasn't far from the seaside
Brest or St Malo

Near the Orient isn't that what you call Sweden and Norway?

Guns are fired in the middle of the night at the German clowns
When the blackness arrives
In the shedding of love tears I write you in black blood

Then there are happy tears in the sunny central arrondissement

I think I love thee as you might one day love me
a mere sub-lieutenant lathered in gore and kinship
in the dark ducts of war

Gillian Lou Marghareta

Août 1997
After Apollinaire

Memories Are Made Of This

Two licorice lakes
Catcleugh and Kielder
fed with dark burnwater
and Jackie's nightie drying on the line

Garth Hudson opens the intro to Tears of Rage in 1969
And the electric voices make your eyes pop out of their sockets
It is only the small-minded who don't understand and get ploated
In their stupid and square Fairisle sweaters and accordion beards
Because we all dress in the finest Italian from Marcus Price & Nickleby's

When I reached home to The Laurels I admired the blue enamel oven
And there was beautiful Jewess Vivienne in a soft woollen pink suit
But the demons of memory crawled through my body & I couldn't do it
Even though she lay in my double bed all night completely naked
Except for a pair of lilac high-heeled matching
shoes I slept downstairs Soviet & virginal

I was a man in a new-look baggy nightshirt starched and white
Trepanned because of a starreburst in the trenchant trenches
I stood by the window and shaved and shaved away my grievous unrest
Whistling part of Milhaud's Four Seasons which I really don't know that
well
Having only heard it a thousand times It seems like opera to me

You who turn to royalty instead of the ultimate truth of Marxist democracy
And to the true modernism of ideas which Pablo understands so well
There is everything to be said that the Jesus Christ Almighty wants us to
die twice
At least the Germans only invite you once to a rat-swarming grave

Août 97
After Apollinaire

Love's Swanne Song

**It is said that love comes and is the Symphonie Phantastique
As if a song which has passed down the centuries
A rustling noise of lost kisses now to us the famous lovers in the Odeon
Walking from café to café at the Hôtel de Ville under the darkening sky
We always cry for love Bar and Jac even in the vingtième arrondissement
Even in the shadows of the Communist town hall of which we are proud
The man and womanhood of the two heroes involved the two swannes
The differences are erected like the Eiffel Tower between us like a jetplane
Jason and the Argonauts who cares about him with his wimp lisp
All swannes die but we do not want to die alone and unloved
After we have had the wonderful warmth of the sunne on our wings
And we have swumme in the Elvet and mated forever for life
And until I move it will not be possible for us to move any more
The panthers are moaning and weeping in the jungles of the night
The rumours of our split are deafened by the rising exotic plants
But they rise through through the thickening leaves and I quell them
And see the jetblack panthers and spotted cheetahs and quell them too
The massive artillery will be upon us again today and will astonish
us with its fantastic affection hitting people right in the face and body
We will think of Dunbar's beautiful beaches and the rolling waves where
we swam And the German shells will arrive without postcards**

And in the sky we will hear the song of all of the love ever in the world

After Apollinaire
Août 1997

The Illegal 2CV

At the beginning of August in the year of 1997
I was brokenhearted and bereft by my grey-eyed strawberry blonde
I rose from my bed in Dunbar shortly before the crack of dawne
In a car driven by Kev back from the Buddhism centre

I sat in the back reading the match reports That's fine by me

We stood and watched the flocks of terns leaving England
It was briefly after 5am and I was alive
I was all of a sudden in love with someone else who talked about Jesuse
She used to serve scampi and very good French fries
And Marg
Was in the front seat with her noble nose
She looked like an Empress and of course she is

We said ta-ra to Blackfriars after one coffee

Only hours later a huge flock of terns were sweeping left to right
Their taut tight wings beating the blackening sky

The salmon were rising up the falls into the pools of Wylam
Whole centuries of opposing anger were clashing together
Even the dead were stirring in their quiet slots and I was trembling

Guard dogs barking at every single corner
I walk this earth with every battle honoured in my struggling soule
They rise within me and rise again and I see them twisting through
the mountains and fountains of the defeated town squares of my heart
Through Kielder and the hamlets of Catton where the best eggs are
And Rookhope and Stanhope and by the Banks of the Allen
They come here and rape it and then leave it to die in so-called peace
The flags are out and there is a room and a sky full of brightness

People are getting on their dawn trains and they will die at their
destinations
Once more they wave their morning newspapers like bonny flags
They have come from Blyth where the disease-ridden cod stir the depths
Turned into bloaters already by the great power station tidalturns
Hiding for life in the wreckage areas where ships have gone down
Above the Iraqi desert Geordie boys fight against other airmen
It is quite dizzying to think they fight at such speed
It is much higher than the terns I saw today flying west
It was almost as if they were fleeing the Norway sunne to find the Spanish
one!
I loved their sharp wings and their strange way of flocking
But there was one behind all on its own and its name was Barry
Yob fights yob yes They call it Newcastle city centre
Yet some of us are almost literate and we go from bar to bar
And poetry comes to us and believe it or not we write it down
And hits the earthe like the very tail of an unannounced comet

I still feel You know the power of poetry which arrives like mad

We used to organise trade unions and organise the universe
We stood tall upon the globe and really felt it was ours only
We thought we were laying out the Fenwick's window
And all of the farmers of Hexham would be queuing up for the sale
They would be standing there in their boots dumb with amazement
And the dogs of Carliol Place would be running them ragged

I'll never forget the time the car broke down completely lightless
We were on the old A1 and it was utterly distressing
It was before the war of the spirit between us Before catastrophe

It was after midnight it was one it was two it was three
and then you weren't there it was four and you were not there

We went past Dragonville and Belmont and arrived in Newcastle
And saw we were going to have to go and try & slaughter Germans
We turned in Grainger Street and looked at each other lost for words
This tangerine-coloured Deux Chevaux which I was driving illegally
It had brought us up the A167 to a very different world
We are both big lads and I used to play for Northumberland Schoolboys
The bad news is that we have just been made children again
And I am in a little cot with a bullet in my poet's elegant head

Août 97
After Apollinaire

The Garden Door is Open On The World

Tonight Pearl shines beautifully and there is only one cloud as a shawl
as the rich rowan berries are Christmas red and will soon be autumn
yellow and the leaves will fall like strange rain
But Pearl and me will understand We have been there so many times
At the East Allen River the magpies bobbed and nodded sucking hen eggs
And we shot them with a .303 up here called a woman gun
Just to make sure that with the bacon from Nichol's farm we saved some
And then I took you tickling trout and we exchanged fastfingers
And the eye glances were quite astonishing one after the other
The snipe with one wing flies in a circle and then falls to the ground
I think we had better telephone its grieving mother
We are all in a terrible state birds and beasts and lousy poets
There is weeping in the branches and we are all doing it over Gran
The stupid Quayside accountants wipe the sweat with crass ties
I say raise the blind raise the dead raise the halt and lame
We walk into light through the open windows in the café
And the light is built by a series of ingenious insects
Then beauty fell upon us all A cobalt mantle indigo endless
Rescue will come eventually I hope Midnight always at hand
The time when Robert Johnson stepped on the bus
I remember your pairs of shoes under the tallboy
Especially the golden sandalettes you bought for Rachel's wedding
Pearl wandered the marigold beddes unheard by the world
She was entirely in black because she was disgraced in the Allen Valley
by the strange policemen of Jesus from the parish committee
We sat beneath the creaking trees loving our life away before love
The big rammes at Hexham are doing what they do best ramming
So the ewes have gone berserk up on the top fields aching to be tupped
And the green plovers are sweeping over the new pasture and calling
Where Sammy the poacher has brought home even more fresh rabbits
Which he unveils from the darkness of his Methodist overcoat
And being the good lad in the family I get the rabbit's kidney on Sunday
O Toronto where the blowing snow is beautiful but makes us
think it's spring with fresh buds O Newcastle in steamy summer
From the rowan to the holly high up on the Kielder banks it goes
Paris Monterey Nice Cannes Bordeaux and Saint Mark's Place
and the brilliant sunny beaches and crescents of tremendous Antigua
There is a clementine outside of the window facing west
It is the sunne It is the sunne It is the unbroken daylight whatsoever
sunne

Big Mac
Août 1997
After Apollinaire

Forget About Her She Does Not Exist

for Stephen Bierley

Morning again
And the rain falls into the trenches of the hearte
The artillery has been blown to bits
We are blitzed and bombed sorted and invaded
But resisting everything
all the shards of attempted broken spirit
Fight back against the invasions which attempt to smash Thee
When You think nowt remains
There is an inner strength which flies like a seagull or partridge
Fast from the thickness of the heather or the edge of the Farnes
Into the wildness of the Aire
It is only September
yet mornings delay their coming
And there are no summer days in England again
You can tell this by the big rivers dry
as my mouth
I worry about the salmon and the spawning beds for this new season
Rain belts down upon the chocolate peppermint and flowering lemon balm
O Jesuse
What shall we do against the conquests and attacks
There is only one God and he has turned his back against us
September 7am and still almost dark
What is happening to the world

Come on lads! Come on! Up out of those camp-beds!
We must quell the enemy and destroy them.
We must not mistake the Milky Way for the shells which light our night!
Dim the lamplights: Don't give the snipers a target
at which to fire.
Listen: There will be a time when once again We see the snowy owl
and the red buzzard
clawing the beautiful trees
on the Dordogne
and high in the
olive groves

The beautiful grey volcanic rocks still belong to us
They are ours
Remember your loved ones
And if we are defeated your children will be killed
or held in capture
Or gassed if you are of the wrong racial quality
What a joke

No joke lads
We must punish and fashion all of them into deathe
No quarter

Poet Yes
But I weare a starre in my hearte
and I want you to see it
and follow me through the barbed wire
Ignoring the smoke
I wish to slaughter the enemy
just as I need to write poems
There is absolutely no difference

It is like love
The desire for victory will never die

Under death and fortitude
And the terrible clouds of invasion which never winne
Against all of this beautiful freedom already in the world

Septre 97
Inspired by Apollinaire

Please Can Anyone Tell Me Where I Find Love?

I wanted to paint a hearte
in the steame of the bathroom mirror
Because I'm so stuck on you
shaving and the heart-steam idea came to me

I did my Elvis trance walk and felt much better
I did my Eddie Cochran crash act
My Buddy Holly Otis Redding show
That's a small jet buried in snow
That's Ricky Nelson in Rio Bravo
That's another plane with no propeller in the wheatfields
That's Lynyrd Skynyrd laid out and burned
That's Frank with bourbon in his hand
That's a black taxi around the lamp post
That's a French poet with his head stoved in
That's a dead disinherited princess with two future kings
That's a dictionary with the word trepanned in it
I still don't know where to find love
I went to Florac
Las Vegas too
I sat upon 1400 toilets
And haven't found it yet
I saw a woman in a mask
Who couldn't say No and Yes

We did the Elvis trance dance and felt like elks in the
treeline

We rode a Motor Guzzi California
All the way from Alston Moor
She fell asleep on the back seat in her biker's jacket
and green cord jodphurs
hugging me like mad
and still we survived
And when we got home
We did the Elvis dance trance but this time we did it in bed
There was love
on the carpet
Love on the floore
There was creamy love
Up against the doore

No I want people to see us do it I don't care
She said
Brazen beyond belief and increased by lack of love

We went to a North Yorkshire village hall
dancing the night away
And did the Elvis trance dance heel and toe and high fives before invented
She was in a red silk suit with pearl Bordeaux shoes
Making all the locals nervous

We left at four in the morning
leaving the pond ducks screaming

The bed broke almost when we arrived back
Honey 110 miles an hour on and off the road
was as much as we could do

We sped home to the bathroom mirror on the burgundy carpet
And everything happened

TAKE ME TO HEAVEN   you said   first time

Then we did the Elvis scrawl the crawl the Elvis drive lick and slide
And tongue-fingered drawl
Honeybunch
Honeybabe
Your blackpants rippedoff
Baby   I love you   in the bus station
In your left ear before the coach to Richmond
You said you liked it
Green courts

Ankles like wine
Tuscan
In a slightly swaying glass
Down that long corridor
From one end to the other

And yet I seek a swanne's eternal love
I wish to close the jailhouse door
I've served my time
and so have you

We waved our funny parts in the Elvis trance dance

And we were orgasm-bound

We were skying upwards and towards new peaks

Our Elvis pelvises
shuddered and shook
We took
Love Off the hook
But Where is Love

Today?

Septre 97 after Apollinaire

The double bone in the throat of the street

Standing before one of the cathedrals my face in the dirt
I won't touch her with a Chinese bargepole
She wears white silk stockings and white courts but smokes
sHe cAsts a shadow longer than the barrel of a steel handgunne
It has more power than a .303
now that autumn has arrived & leaves are falling
& the rowan berries have turned cherry red at last
as if it was Christmas
She buys her shoes at Next
I'm shocked
She'd be better off at Scope the cancer shoppe

Cherie
Comme Je t'aime
Twentieth arrondissement

Communiste seulement –
I love you and your Swiss chard stalls!

We walk through Bastille
and I am once again a poet
Inspired by the Guillotine
and we scorch up les guimauves
Yarmouth bloaters
I've been in a world drink & drugs
I've been in space you've
never seen
Guns in shaky hands
Gin & whisky & Wives & funny behaviour
Forgive me Lord I didn't mean mean business

Lord this is what I meant
I had an outpouring of love
I wanted
to pour it out
but Did not know
to whom I should purr it

I sank and sacrificed myself a thousand times

Ten thousand timeS

Four thousand times
She has been a beauty all of my life
She has been a beauty every day
She cleaved her heart
to me and I betrayed her
at 3.27am in Percy Street
Nine thousand times
Ten Thousand times

After the Club A Gogo
3.28
Give Me Back the Ring

Dark-haired Catherine

I have payed for it
one million Times

Septre 97e
after GUILLAUME

At The Hoppings

for Anthony and Fiona

after Apollinaire

Steel tricks bust our skulls
They're elegant bright & smash us in
Make them Go on then German engineer

The fight between grace and bravery

Black Swiss ski-pants
Rising livewire over the barbed wire
Like a white silk Northumberland Street Fenwick bra that you unhook
There isn't a moment like it
I LOVE IT THE WHITENESS OF cloudes
Write it on my headstone

Poets stalking Kielder
Through larches and other abstract trees
I've known you so long since Buxton Indifference Is a stranger
His plucky gunne almost stops me dead
Even the withering roses give hope to my hearte
Then I go to hospital and don't know my heade

Because I dream of the roses of other places
Where they bloom unblemished by headwounds
O my love O my love O my great verity Thee also a rose
Dollywobbles Your hips spread out widc

I breathe alcoholism into the air
Then the starres and argent sky swoon through my filters
And the shells hit our skulls
This beautiful trenchwater This gorgeous meadow
Stricken by artillery

I rise up in polished black boots
Which I polished myself because we received supplies

The roses are dead and we die too

But the roses will eventually winne

Septre 97
Just before the Hellhound Train Never Ending Tour
From Guillaume's Fête

I'm Doomed To Love You Forever

You forgot
Paris
You forgot the train tunnel
You didn't remember the thousands of candles in Sacre Coeur
flickering in the breath of the nun's singing
You forgot the Ile de la Cité

You forgot everything

I'm doomed to love you until the day I die
Our relationship never goes onward
I'm doomed to love you forever

From Mars to the Bethlehem starre
From the Milky Way to big black holes
I saw the comets and I am doomed to love you forever

I cannot move the earth
I have tried
I have always been a union man
But I am destined to love you forever

I try to find new loves
But I am doomed to love you forever
They are mere ghosts compared to Thee

And when I am in my braindead state
forgetting everything except the last Newcastle result
or Paris St Germain
Or how the directors of my clubs
will always come a cropper

I am doomed and damned to love you forever
Just as Columbus wanted the new
world

Now I'm lost

Absolutely
Please leave me a hole to fit in

Lost and with a hole in my helmet

We must live to win

I am Doomed to Love You Forever

Septre 97e
After Toujours by Apollinaire

I Don't Walk The Line All of The Time

You don't know what
You don't know what
You don'tknow fuckall
You don't know the fall
back from the brink
The journey from the ball
to the endless drinke
Get a load of it
,my children
I'm flat out loaded
If the logs fall from the fire
I'll burn to death
Sacrifice a final breath

Autumn now and the leaves are falling like poems
onto the pages of the pavements
War is everywhere and the dead are dead or dying
And the conspiracies
Never cease
They lie on crispest sheets white and blue
Where is my brother tonight

I long for him to be well and better
and care not for myself
I give up my own care
I collapse it into the earthe
I balloon it to the sky
That he should leave the trenches of his inner-war
I don't care
Yes I do
Because I love a woman very special
She wears a mustard shirt
I touched it even
Cherise denims and brown sandals
Those little toes pointing out

Peachy Tremendous Absolutely Splendid

A bonus like Rain

Septre 97 After Guillaume

All of Your Sinnes Will be Known Always And Never Forgiven

The seamist has risen from the Arctic roses and from the lemon balm
and is now replaced by the bright Northumberland sunshine of August
Long live France I say or you'll end up in a bed dead and then a coffin
And who wants to be a stiffo in the Père Lachaise in the 20th
next to Edith Piaf Oscar Wilde and that strange bloated man bad poet Jim Morrison
But all of your sinnes are known by Jesus and unless you renounce them
you will never be in a position to stalk the earth and tell a poet's truth
I sleep in my wee bed of a soldier facing death from rifle and Zeppelin
I do not want to lie next to the bullet holes which slaughtered the Communards
I'd prefer to die in the arms of my beloved heroine Lou who also speaks poetry
Yet trepanned I am grateful to Doctor Brennan who brought me back to life I will be eternally
dedicated to Sister Susan with her blue uniform & white strategic gloves
Now that I have gone awry crooked askew lopsided off-centre unsatisfactory
And hammer the hardmetal of the streets without completing my various responsibilities
Except spitting in the gutter at the former headmaster who tried to pederast me
There are times when you don't complete
And later it is a long time of regret   Pablo speaking of me on his death-bed

to be finished
due to complete exhaustion
Au 97
after the main man

Petition to the Jesus Christ Almighty

Just a bairn
And I stalked the back lanes of Walker
opposite the Neptune Naval Yard
with my little camera
and blue overalls with straps
destined for fame
Even then I spoke to the Virgin Mary as a friend
and said my prayers at night before blessed sleep
and the latest round of shelling
And asked Jesus to love me forever
I knew I would love Thee till I die a swanne
And yet the endtime has appeared like a bomb
but I do not believe in the cerulean blue of Italian heaven
or the infinite crimson of German shellhole hell
I cast my beliefs aside I cast aside all doctrines and philosophies
I will never subscribe to anything ever again except charcoaled flags
The seaman who was picked up in the choppy waters
off the Black Middens
starved freezing and hungry but near the headquarters of the NUS
because he always wore a cross and silently said his prayers
He looked like me he looked like me he was me

after Apollinaire
Août 97

Annie

At the shores of Whitley Bay
Between the Black Middens and Blyth
My huge garden overgrown and cascading with Victorian tea roses
My gorgeous little house
a tremendous overblown rose in itself
O darling I miss your letters from Hollywood

And our pony-tailed dances in the Methodist hall

Often you stalked elegant and alone
among the roses of the church garden
And I passed gazing after you
longing and longing for love of you
longing and longing for your dancing feet
We looked at each other Annie as if there was no tomorrow

O Annie don't join the Methodists
for God's sake
Look at the rosetrees and leave on your buttons
and don't become a Menonite
There is only one law no clothes for lovers   And shells and war
If you are going to take off your buttons
join me in some strange club
One's just dropped off my new Nickleby's reefer jacket
does that mean we worship the same Christ?

There is nothing grimmer than this grim darkest of nights
except perhaps Mons
There will be nothing darker than endless and relentless as death itself
The German tracers will never stop until all my comrades do

after Apollinaire

I Love You But No

One night is enough in London
Fenwick's and the Tate mist and fires of the heart
Soho gayboys run towards the taxi we repel them
But the strange looks make me lower my eyes in despair
I am beside myself for want of Thee whom I think almost perfect

There was a rentboy waiting for a Conservative MP
He used to be a member of the Cabinet not the rent boy
But he used to bugger him so in fact they were joined in a particular manner
Old Compton Street and the Italian wine shops were
like the Red Sea ready to be parted

They're bringing down parts of Benwell brick after brick
I don't understand how you do not cling to my love
having lived so long in the halls of Hell but not as long
I swept grandly through my very own for a decade
I was a stark pyramid under the sunlight of Margaret's magnificent Egypt

I stood alone in the Groat Market with the surrounding white dresses
and chunky heels and flares   That burned the night sheer alight
Next to the Pizza Express the Grainger Street experiment
was coming to fruition a city sore being mended
Jac might have a bad fallen arch but she'll be alright in time with care

I saw the wreckage of human and mortal love – not Blakean –
approach me like a broken open wound and it hit me in the face
It crept upon me like a German dog it felt my neck and kissed my throat
It arrived like a silken parachute onto a wheatfield in dead of night

I stood by the blazing fire with Chaucer my tricolour hound
He was as unruly as me He wouldn't take any orders at all
That's the way a poet's dog should be But my current partner
the swanne works a singular loom and makes it work like Morris

I am her swanne her stag her wild thing within the driveway
Her instructions hammered the brightness of my Tyneside skies
She drove me from the stricken bowls of Durham to the end of my days
You search the earth sometimes right along the A19 from Station Town

And all you find is an abyss which really is worse than Shildon
I would sell my whole soul Jac for one kiss from Thee I would
Otherwise why did we go to Paris on Le Shuttle it was a marvellous time
Others have unmixed souls but as you say ours are pearl and plain

My happiness is a nothing a zero My fake attitude is a bottom line
Sometimes you pursue a black Ford Zephyr and end up finding Hell
I lie back in the snows of memory and think of you despite it all
from the sweetness of the roundabout pick-up to the darkest night

2

Scorched earth policy razed whole cities and forests to the very ground
We scattered communities from every corner of the earth
We went from one place to the other making them ours without quarter
O Bounty Bar sky you look so dark chocolate and utter milky

Goodness the white stockings and the white Fenwick knickers
are certainly an attraction My poet's voice rang with poetry
It is getting dark already and yet only the month of July
The guns spirit away the darkness of what used to be called eternal night

We follow the leader whoever that is and hang in there hard
Thinking it's a good idea and also good for the heart at the time
My dawn delight my wonderful woman my non-fear of meeting love
Singing and talking in the magpie dawn we were toes twined it seemed forever

She who was my queen my warrior queen and beloved comrade
who took the petals of the iris and let me rub them against her clitoris
Who rubbed my cock with the midnight blue petals of the new iris
We twined our twenty toes beyond belief and loved and loved

All gods and diadems are extinct even Elvis Presley The Memphis Flash
Just look Sid Vicious and Nancy Spungen gone the whole distance
Many are dead and have died and gone to earth The cats stalk and I weep
In Paris however where we just were the gods of art live and live Pablo

I know you you beloved comrade and warrior queen you the tremendous
But you keep confirming it is an elegy now a complete thing of the past
This song of the thrown-over hero who walked into your halls of hell
You are the siren of the rocks across the causeway of my life

I shake rattle and roll love is a corpse completely without life
There have been idols women men and especially Jerry Lee and
High School Confidential and of course Heartbreak Hotel
and High Heel Sneakers and the gold suit on the cover of that album

Me I lap like a true hound at the stream of my creamy dreames
I wander in the valley of her breasts like Byron with club-foot mind
I cling like an ivy to the oak of her stern pushaway hearte
I am the unbelieved courtier at her queendom I am the servile servant

Barrabas you tosser you wanker you bastard you complete fuckface
You have the devil's horned face with a massive cavern in his heart
Keep feeding on your 666 smut pornography filth and trash
We will not we will not we will always resist your badly-cooked lunches

You thief relieved by the massive covenant of the crowd as hands were washed
We don't need you you could have saved the Jesus Christ Almighty
You could have sacrificed your life for the great Elvis Presley
O Northern Starre which I can see all the way to the causeway at Lindisfarne

3

Northumbria is surely and I mean forever the Promised Land
The complete home of women in white walking down Northumberland Street
They are starres as well in the universe looking for similar attractions
Listen vamp your North Sea eyes are sweeping like a broken firmament
They reflect the skies the wild skies like a jet panther in the jungle

Darling my love I know you want to catch a jet from Newcastle to Florence
My dearest love it will be a surprise when we go there kisses and fine coffee
You'll remember your mother and we wept like violins dusk to dawn
When she looked at me after the County I could barely then appreciate

her wonderful look But I have to say my real care is to see you again
My Jackie My Jackie My Jackie My Jackie My absolute Jackie
Don't go with anyone else don't go with anyone else be a swanne don't betray me
I will live forever on the Blackwellgate Bridge if it means you'll come back to me

The Elvet swims with fastwater from up a height and raining
and I will weep and pray with gladness at seeing her again
My blocked head my starved heart will empty into a sky empty of pain
Your children Rachel and Ben sing so happily yet we are separate and sad

I pray in the middle of these lonely nights that I never forget Thee
My pouchy pigeon my tumbler my beautifully-breasted dove
My white cliffes of Dover my Folkestone Harbour my ferry landing
My Isle of Skye my box edged like lace headed with whiteness

I am the Pooka I will dance in the Club a Gogo listening to Muddy Waters
I will stride across the Erith Marshes like Magwitch in the darke
And I will call upon all of the locusts of Israel to drop from the heavens
And eat their way through Gallowgate and eat out the eyes of the dead

In death you die but there will be pain and there will be extra pain
Where the soul shakes rattles and rolls flips flops and flies
From the A167 where the white-dressed and tattooed dollies
are eventually heading for death I hate to say arrayed with single red roses

God to me is nothing more than gamboge wallpaper from B&Q
You have sent the man in black to exorcise Pearl of her muteness
And you wicked ministers failed and should remove your buttons
Your strict instruction your downfall your obstruction to a well of light

Your religion is not true religion it is a mixture of guns and lies
You want me to die I won't die until I've finished my mission
I will write through the night until I have ended my so-called mission
You here sometimes and now always there My six-feet shadow by the lemonbalm

Sparty and Alston grass dies in the snows of November and December
The upland robins went wild inside the mysterious borage groves
April will come again and we will all feel well again in the morning
The argent artilleries of snow will melt away and we will live

The unemployed are pleased because their gas bills are smaller
But my hearte my hearte is still as heavy as the feldspar carried by Pearl
from the tumblestones past the Castrol-treated stile to Sipton Shield
And now there are seven wounds in my side Seven wounds for every year

4

O my heart I did not understand why my first poem was rejected
by my jealous father My heart my heart was heavy as stone
Already I had loved too much I loved into the future I was a nuisance
completely to myself I was alone in the universe even before I went to New York

The Tyne is a great river bronze and gold in the windows of the morning
When the young women of Newburn splash themselves in the summer evening
Undressed almost like goddesses and the scullers' songs are wind on the water
They follow the breeze all of the way from the coast of Donegal to Stella Power Station

The Catholic candles in Saint Basilique and under my appletree
where the winds from Bedlington and Blyth and Penrith and Dunbar
fly in from every side and the logs go on and Pearl says hello
All of the night is furnace of feast sex and endlessly relentless flame and fire

We are completely crazed by the baked wild bird you made just for us
With the Northumberland potato and the leeks and the shank of sheep
Both wives left you it was probably your fault one disappeared forever
One became a social policewoman knocking on doors in the middle of the night

One sat upon my motorcycle in the courtyard in green cord jhodpurs
white socks and recently dyed hair at Saks in Darlington she was the best
We sank into the evening We gave everything up unto the very sky
I do not want to die on the Felling By-Pass but in Paris with Jac or Sue

There are a million Sundays which I will never ever see or speak of
Darn Crook Amen Corner down by The Side in complete madness
I am a sung spitted-outswanne a man whose lover & partner has gonne
I am a pitted olive black from where Shelley died and dead completely

Nights in Paris – 20 times – soaked in Ginievre and various pâtés
in the jazz clubs in the cinemas in the Citroen workers' factory
The Metro smells like a ghost and I want to introduce you to it
The Metro is like musick from Stockhausen it rocks until one in the morning

Despite everything I have given my heart and loved you so well
The halls of Hell have been a thing of the past for years now
We do not wish to be thrown to the fishes at the Newburn tidal mark
Your wonderful poems will be the last great thing I understand and know

Juillet 97 /Mars 98
after Apollinaire's
Le Mal Aimée

Entrance to Heaven

The door of the Hotel Armstrong grins like an insomniac maniac
In the decent and quiet avenue of the Communist 20th arrondissement
Where we are falling completely in and out of love again darling
Mam what does this mean for me other than a trip towards death
Wylam rail bridge so far away now and the salmon spawning beds
just upstream from the Rocket Angling Club's private fishing banks
She became an icy angel an advocate of winged sensibility
I still listen to her lips on the telephone singing her distant song
Just for love of it and then it and my heart dies and dies
I am abashed cheapened devalued and completely debased
I am an arrow-ridden zero on the last pub dartboard in Alston
I am in the Angel Inn and not one cherub will speak to me
The German artillery at least want to communicate wounding death
Listen Bar I taught you to read and write opposite the Neptune Yard
At the age of three and four the rest of the world is poetry so live & work

After Apollinaire
Août 1997

Wylam Railway Bridge

Here where the Tyne flows from the wonderful uphills
                and you fling your arms out in your waxed jacket on our
Suprematist structure
I remember and remember and it's like a Willie Nelson song of utter regret
                                And it's my persistent qualm and affliction
Happiness and boon times have gone forever

Come on darkest night and raise your fists in my face
Hit that bell hit that bell I'm standing here ready for anything and nothing

O we held hands and twined our fingers so very keenly
And we stood on the bridge and faced each other like no tomorrow

And we twinned and twined and kissed in our hearts at Kielder Dam
Up the dale and up the valley
                    We lapped like the tidal turn down at Blayney Row
The stag from the treeline and the doe from the bowl of Durham
                    Staring towards each other from the boughs of the larches

        Let the night give me its eight pound gloves & hammer me in the jungle
        The days will pass and I may rise again from the doctor's couch to live

Let these darkest nights frag me to smithereens while I break into a jigsaw
Heart kinship love and cherishment run away faster than the Tyne

It flows and flows away all the way from Haltwhistle to the tidal turn
But the rest of life is ponderous throttled and jammed solid no coping
                                Hope is wrested from its miserable station
And not one person especially her can tell you anything about it

        Let night come and dawn and I will be here right on guard gloves on
        And will seek thee and seek thee and always wear you ring of blue

Each day races like a flood and then the months of sheer psychosis
        But our times darling cannot be caught in a net again like an owl
                    Except you said our souls are knit and I believe it
Our pink salmon spawning beds lie under the Wylam railway bridge
And our Tyne flows the hills and madly away

        Let the darkest night hit me like Ali in his finest hour
But I will stand here as best I can to defend the broken love of we

Août 97
After Apollinaire

The DollBird/Redblonde

after Apollinaire

I stand in front of you all despite it all I'm still sensible, straight-tongued
I understand everything about life and death because I've been
and am still on the fringes of both
Two wives and a million women one after the other
I convinced others notably newspaper employers and union colleagues
to follow my way of thinking and then it seems I suddenly failed
I know French, some Italian, no German, who would want to
except to appeal to them to stop shooting their monumental artillery
I have been in a million places: Paris, the Cevennes,
Cannes, Gloucester, Massachusetts, St Mark's Place with the
late Allen Ginsberg but never Denver Colorado
I was wounded in the head in the heart in the soul of the mind
and went on the drip because of the alcoholism which hangs my brain
I lost everyone Allen Ed Mark they all went the complete distance
The people I unkindly wanted to go wouldn't leave this earth
I did not have a gunne it was hopeless I wanted them to go NOW
I will have to detach myself from this warre between thee and me
I will have to disattract myself from your 4 lipstick prints on the walle
There is a great notice in the Sky: this is the order this is the new idea
I had this terrible moment of shame I couldn't remember his name
then it returned like a flurry of gunfire I was abashed in forgetfulness
You think you speak in God's words I don't think so
When you've been on the Heminevrin drip you really do know better
the entyre universe
you wait all night long for people to die replaying Hank Williams in your
brainbox
Swan Hunter asbestosis victims
men from the shut collieries
Unknown bonfires of the heart
Rainbows never seen
Unrenounced dreams of Clare

Kindness will be investigated and hopefully a newly-peaceful country
We will retrieve time
we will not

We're on the borders night and day shooting at enemies we do not know
it is the end of time and the time of the future
at the same time
Pity us
Pity us
our mistakes are as big as our terrible sinnes

The relentless upheavals of summer come upon us with Pearl in the
meadows of Sparty
some say it is a time of violence with the bursts of the flowers
my childhood lies in tatters beneath the apple trees

O my darling sunshine wake before me let me sleep
my springtime as in Milhaud is corrupt completely
I thought reason had a chance but now I know better

I'm waiting sweetheart I think your name is Kelly
I'm hanging about to follow the sweetest form there is
And you Kelly will walk through the streets of Newcastle
with everything hanging off you like antlers

And every night I will be magnetised to your bedroom
The dollbird with the square high-heels and the ruby locks
Her hair is argent it is so brisky frisky and buoyant
A torchlight a lighthouse going on into eternity

Victorian tea-roses from the garden which haunt
the world with their hearth and heartlike flames

They never fade in a paradisial slow parade of death
They have always an eternal sweetness of nature's breath

Go on take the piss all of you take the mick
I know everything and if I told you you'd go the distance
          So many items of a various nature you would not want

Mercy ache tenderness
Unbelievable sanity
lay them in the courtyard at my door

And pity me forever for what I know
                    about everyone and the complete universe

Juillet 97
after Apollinaire

Listen It's Plutting

for Caroline Calvert

Then
l
ist
en
to
the
mus
ick
of
the
fall
ing
rain
so
10
der
so
swee
t

sol
diers
houn
ded
lo
st
in
the
lim
bs
of
a mill
ion
art
illery
hor
ses
be
neath
the
cres
cent
moo
n

of
Flan
ders
o
ur
a
go
ny
under
the
rain
pl
ea

se
rain
stop
eve
n
so
swee
t

con
fuse
the
en
emy
hor
izon
wi
th
gunn
es
th
ough
the
al
most
in
visible
lace
mist
is
so
swee
t t
oo

O
My
Sparty
rain
so
ten
der
my
Dirt
Pot
pluts
you
ta
sty
as
m
y
lo
ve

Horse intestines are spilled on the path
So long gun-trenches
We WILL recover them
we will retrieve the Front
With gun-cunning
As we gaze sadly into the hell shell-holes
Filled with the blood and guts
Of horses and comrades

The Germans have ended the ceasefire
Don't you see We won't come back again
I am thc poct of thc trenche
And dead in the helmethead I will not come back

To the
Pe
ris
co
pe

To check the enemy trenches
We don't want France to die

The Club a Gogo which smashes
the silence of night
with Muddy Waters and Jimmy Reed
Bright Lights Big City

Like the German shells

A wild beck in the sky

Don't stuff the beaks of the birds with child cotton
Don't attract your heart with extra pain
And to the kisser of the flagge
And the walker of miles from Elba
Say
Helllo
He brought France into the modern age
I am France and France is Me!

But as the shelles deluge and spate
Everything is demented now
Here where we lads are

Septre 97/Mars 98
After Apollinaire

Letter From Guillaume Apollinaire to Barry MacSweeney

My dear fellow poet
Life is so difficult you can go from bad to verse
Tonight the German tracers filled the sky like starres
Bar it is a complete tragedy that you are there and I am here
and I am in a rainsodden trench and that you are not
I don't enjoy it believe me I prefer my stylish Paris shoes
striding up to Montmartre to have a chat with Pablo my best mate
O goodness Bar the bombardments have begun again it's pouring down on the trenches
You're dead lucky only the North Sea mist is seeping in on you
Out here beyond Brittanny before ferries were invented
we are under the Bosch cosh
fantastically thickened to the very earth of the universe
And once more the tracers fill my eyes like the skies
and like the orange lights beneath the tyres as you walk along Rookwood Road
My fellow poet
don't despair at the non-appearance of your book
you know that it will appear one day
We may both be dead
but the lights in the sky
and the brilliant shadows under the wheels
of these tremendous modern cars

In the trenches

Secret Poem Number Nine

for SJL

I questioned – on the first time we made love – whether you
trimmed your quim hair and you said no –
And I have always thought you a complete idol ever since
You are like a female Elvis Aaron to me under a Graceland sky
I'm a crackerjack a wacky Jacky myself chopping down women
O my 4 red lipstick kissprints on the wall of my study
What am I carp in your pond a trout in your running becks and streams?
You my gong my siren my bells of St Mary The Kindred
I have walked the snowladen peaks all of my life looking for thee
You are the snow-filled hills and fells and the law of Alston
I seek your wonderful mouth with my gorgeous bow and arrow
And you will be my darling collector of silk & steel flesh
I will use my crampons to haul myself into your sun-brightened hairlocks
You are the various swivelling spit vessels on the canals of my kisses
And the lily we brushed against each others' intimate most personal parts
In the most erotic moment of our now broken lives
O my apple and pear trees are filling with good fruit
And the sweet suckling of your breasts
under your bra gone for good from one broken blue guitar string to another
There is a light in the sky almost a torch of sheer flame
And it is a zero pronouncement it is a useless arrangement we don't even have
A retirement from life a doomed cult Lipstick traces now only no Yes sir none Sir!
The kind of Tarantino quarantino beloved by medics
Blood guts brains on the ground no love ever again Only war

Juillet 97/Mars 98
after Apollinaire

1997

My eternal love – the one who tells me our souls
are knit
wears a fantastic lilack silk suit from New Bond Street
bought especially for a trip to a poetry reading in Devon
And she wears those gold sandalettes bought for Rachel's wedding

Her eyes prom flirt flutter and waltz like cherubs
She laughed and giggled in the café
La Tourelle   plats du jour
Our hearts and toes were I thought forever twined
The complete colours of Paris fled into our hearts
It was the revolution all over again
The guillotines and the knitting were in our very minds
The wonderfully useful cobblestones

As we stayed in the vingtième arrondissement
the only Communist one in Paris
Stephen says
What a pure choice

Her lilac suit with its fresh collar
Hair done at Fenwick's
Arms swathed in brilliant sunlight and Verlaine rain

We never heard midnight we were in the Hôtel de Ville

She trailed the boulevards in those golden shoes
And I fell in love with her again and again
and again
Up the Tower
into the atmosphere of the clouds

She is foxy, peachy, magnificent gorgeous beyond belief
I dared to love her and she broke my heart

There have been some horrendous encounters in tremendous cities
With the throngs of new children
Iron and steel in the veins
but at least complete flamebrains
I loved 1968 the Citroen workers showing me car parts
In the shelves ready to throw at gendarmes
Everything is useless like beauty and luxuriants

She is so gorgeous
She terrifies me

*

Juillet 97
After Apollinaire

The Vows

For Pablo

We came to your museum in the ancien école
it was absolutely sensational sensational beyond belief
We just managed to enter before the visitors from California
And we could not leave the bull from a bike saddle and handlebars for
example or the teeth of the Spanish goat-head's cavernous nostrils
And the guitars and African women why should we leave?
At dawn it plutted outside the Hotel Armstrong
We trawled the rooms and saw the women of Avignon
It was completely and absolutely amazing
There was a strange excitement with the woman whose eyes were near her
breasts
Eyes akin to her navel
Lemon grove babes are falling in love in their sexy sling-backs
Blue and black Dusty eyeliner like the larches at Kielder
where we stared and stared over the coriander soup brought in a Thermos
Their hearts are noosed like the lemons of your beloved Spain

*

Pity? Like Pearl I have none in my wallet
And my withdrawal and silence is a complete affliction
All of my poems have been altered into a firmament
And Adam is rising from Blake's visionary copper plate towards the sunne of
my eyes
And as a carrier of sunnes I am sultry torrid and acute
What have I done to the Biblical brutes and beasts
The ones who have broken down from lapsed intelligence
Once upon a time the mortified used to spring awake and long for me
And then I looked forward to the End Time just like Bob
But now mine is arriving courtesy of the unmollified German Empire
and I will soon be laid out on a strange slab
washed with a doctor's peculiar liquids and coined in a slot

*

I've been well brave   I returned to the past
The very slabself of my longlostdays
My path scattered with rubbish I'm mourning in the morning
It's amazing there are some in the Basilique St Denis
She lies there with her last exhalations
Or is still a fragrant one in the lemon groves
A complete petal giving the fig of her body
On others day we cried alone like Willie Nelson
and died bereft in solitary drinking places
Watching the poppies in the passing gardens fan out like flames
And the blue roses of the flashed-out fuse explode
In the allotments of my memory

Your betrayals no longer send shivers up and down me
That Pearl moon again a total omelette
A righteous poached egg on a Parisian plate
The bangle the brooch of dew is in memory of the bathing beauty
who fell asleep in the water
And here darling my bunch of Passion petals
And a crown of thorns to remind you of the Jesus Christ Almighty
It's been raining I do not mind at all

In this house the excellent angels of Jesus & Elvis Aaron are at work at once

The lunartick sadness will evaporate eventually
Each day is a holy one
St Michael stalks the stairs
I walk I sing the man called Cash
There was a woman once who leaned from a window
in French we say fenêtre
and she gazed into my eyes it seemed forever her name was Karen
After we kissed I walked away my heart like a violin played by a hero
Who always wins his war against the blankest canvas

after Apollinaire
Juillet 97

Fancy Nancy

Germaine hello! What a smashing Fenwick skirt
It's a frock fit for a democratic princess
even though you're cruel and an independent solicitude
Let me stroke it   silk from mysterious Japon
Hand-made and trimmed with Chantilly lace

Your beautiful skirt is a silken chime and siren
whose double clapper – your wonderful legs – have
struck the passing of my romantic fancies
O Germaine Karen I ring that bell my chest heaving
with an ardour a real purpose to stroke your white-stockings

Your tall Waddington Street bedroom O my clamour
is a belfry in itself ringing moans and cries
My eager fingers stroke your silk and it tears my one good ear
Those wonderful legs in Gallowgate on which your skirt flows like a river
And these Villonesque men hung from the gallows are amazing my eyes

The little boatlight on the top of your wardrobe is still as the night

Juillet 97
after Apollinaire

For Rachel Levitas, The Finest Painter in England

Henri the Customs Officer was perhaps as great as Thee
But I doubt it on the banks of the Seine
He didn't have your imagination
Or your Blakean breadth
Which I love beyond belief
Dear Rachel
I greet you
                                        Delaunays
We pass through the Customs House of heaven
And when we rise to Zion we will bring you fresh brushes
and new tubes of paint and brilliant white canvases
So that in the cornflower expanses
you can devote your time
your Communist leisure
in the very true light of life
To painting
St Anthony
his wild-winged temptations
and the   everlasting starres

Juillet 97
after Apollinaire

Rue Christine Lundi

Nation, The Square of the Overturned Throne
Where we put the guillotine
It's far more than we did in England
Except once which was not enough
The Hotel Armstrong in Communist 20th arrondissement where you can buy
harrisa opposite the street market filled with beautiful fresh vegetables
And it was like a honeymoon even though we are not married
Keep the stile open while Pearl climbs through
and flitflights her way to the borage groves

We have electricity at last in the Loaning Head
It's been connected
And now you can read we can read together at night
The owner of the beautiful café is gasping for breath
I went to Tunis with a woman I thought beautiful until I met Thee

and I recognised personal wonderfulness for the first time
I bought red hot peppers next to the Rue Bourgiba
and kept them for years
but when I met Thee
you were hotter than Africa
It might be a fascist place but it has a lot of style

In the Hotel Armstrong the Germans are holding up the queues
And the coffee is lukewarm and sour
But the rain of Paris is sweet and you are writing your best poems

We're leaving at 9.15
And I'm most protective of my absolute heart
Which I wish to save for you

There's a mirror in the bathroom of the Hotel Armstrong
Which reminds me of Tyneside and Vickers
There's a mixed-up confusion between us
You taunting beautifully-breasted scallywag woman

There is a wild spirit in you I try to catch like a kite
My new coat protects me from the chill rain
And the black and white cat is stalking the floor

The buns and blueberry cheese were tremendous
And in Alston the taps are running waiting for us
But I don't understand black as her nails

The ground is a circus filled with animals
The redhead in the bookshop was abducted and sold to the world

Listen Jac this is serious My love for you is laid down in silver and gold

The train the Tunnel I wrote about for years

We travelled through it and dozed as if it did not exist

The mind in my brain – imagine! – said Can we prod the little maid
towards you No I don't want her I want the best woman poet in England
Her name is Jackie Litherland I stand by it I am its protector

I have bought a painting by Rachel Levitas – the daughter of the best
woman poet alive in England   and am as proud as Punch
The Temptation of St Anthony and I am in it borne aloft by Demons

Stockhausen says   Ignore the known world
I agree
You are the greatest living woman poet in England
so acknowledge yourself
and stand tall in the world
as you should
your absolutely rightful place

Juillet 97
inspired by Apollinaire

The Man who walks

Open the door Richard I'm rocked by continual weeping

The whole of life is strange like the tidalmark at Blayney Row
Just beyond Dunston Staithes and Stella

I was absorbing a monumental cloud on its way to Berwick & Dunbar
which had escaped Pearl's hair
Then the clouds sank into the rim of the law
And disappeared and thankfully it began to rain

We went to Amsterdam to see Malevich the ferry was fantastick
It flew from Harwich like a science fiction film

There were no regrets because the future does not contain them
The waves sped past the cutting bow there were invisible caverns of fish
We realised at once that the Tyne was a flowing part of the whole North Sea
I do remember I do remember I do remember and I miss you

I ran into the duty-free lounge for a big bottle
As we almost arrived in Holland with its endless greenhouses
and its roadside grillhouses with steaks au point

I thought of the Jesus Christ Almighty with his arms like wings
He was flying towards heaven with nails in his wrists
There was an endless array of weird animals and people playing two-card brag
And you – you – had consigned me to the plastic bag of history

Endless moments on Platform 2 at Durham Station soaked in mist
Busy seamen on the ferry it was a very darke time
The women of Amsterdam – dark and of African origin – didn't interest me
I remember everything being not a poet but a cyborg as in a movie
A sailor struck the deck dying from a stroke or heart attack
We rushed there to help but it was absolutely no use

O you my compadres men and women poets in all of the bus stations
Funny automatic hooters as the buses reverse and you're all like me
inventing poems as you wait and walk or go to the Robins Cinema
Then we go to Rushworth and Storey and buy nectarines and don't need to
follow the street signs There aren't any the students have ripped them down
along with the flowerpots
There is a straight regiment of bridges – Leazes and Blackwellgate – harder
to cross than John Wayne in She Tied A Yellow Ribbon
And the Bigg Market up the road on the A1 heaved like a crazed woman
The silver birches swept around under Pearl's moon like a wild wand
And we listened with the window slightly open to the death of summer
To the pies and daws barking in the glorious dawn of the day
And the eternal sounds of the salmon runs over the edge of the Wear and the
weir

The Flass Vale is a mile from the river but is quiet and peaceful
And you wouldn't catch me in Sunderland at the Stadium of Light

But the brilliance of Rookhope is undeniable and Ireshopeburn
Where the shadows gather like passing strangers and then move on
And the clouds yet still on the way to Dunbar rise like impalements

Those brilliant shadows against the sandstone hill where the swifts live at Sipton Shield
Sometimes you know they leaned over lower than we did even though we were small
Striding across the law like a Vulcan bomber going to Otterburn Ranges

Sam the Poacher was a grizzled ghost haunting the nights of our lives
I only see them now in the sepia collection of old photos
Nothing can ever be retrieved
We slept there Annie and you said you liked the lamb broth

That shows you
Life is as unsure
as the tidal mark at Blayney Row
when North Sea waves rush in unbidden
dark as lead seems and equally mysterious

97
after Apollinaire

Treasure

For SJ Litherland

Always long time live my undying love
A princess of golden hair ashblonde
In which nation? I don't know darling.
Long time past lives my love long time
Cost of exotic fruit forever your enemy
It will alter the treasure of your beauty
If we let it, long time my gorgeous lover
My princess of the bullion bargol

There is treasure buried under the earth
The mere cost of the iris petals we rubbed
Tries to temper our beauty quite lately
Through Irish cloakclasps discovered in peat
Beauty's eye plutting alone in the sad rain
She cries she weeps she oars without solace
In a Spanish king's ransom buried under sand
And it is the time of the rubbing of the iris petals

Of your downy moss I am the dawning fire
Murmured and murmuring to the bed queen
Merle song, chant of the whisperer, sunriselark
Your foam beaches against the rough grain of my chin
Hair twined and turned in electric blue forget-me-nots
Such poverty! Yet you're a wonder among all women
I am the ticket collector of your hanky-wiped tides
Green-breasted plovers upon your royal tongue

This is by a young man – 24 – and devoted to you
Who will be handkerchiefing your drying-up eyes
How did the fairy of morning reply to the ring-ousel?
Beside the brave harpist who is nailed to your heart
Who your daughter says She thinks the world of you
Beside us you despise the Aurora Borealis of gold
By the eternal mod in pressed pants who adores you
And who dedicates his life to stop you crying anymore

Ten years of celibacy I waited princess JacLou
Then one day she telephoned and we laughed & laughed
Horsewoman through the empty collieries whip-stirruped
– ten years waiting for the Leveller pizza gossip talker –
Plucky, advancing of the heart, rich without venal cash
Who plundered the stark booty of my heart took it for hers
Ten years in monkish dereliction before Palace Green
Then it was her day her favour on my jousting lance

The poor darling three years in the Halls of Hell
Lovecask wrapped in a purse of dried leather;
The poor darling even though Midlands sensible
So lovable but not loved decently & quite invisible.
One-night sad plunderers boasting invincibilities
Tried to take the purse and boast it their stupid own
The woman in the Halls of Hell would not have it
And the loveflagon remained her own integrity & charm

She wept because of the bondaged body she slept in
But you know it was not necessary to cry day or night
The perils of North Sea winds dislodged the slates
– She would moan and weep in a state of physical indenture –
One man thought he could enter the house causing carnage
But he was nothing but a one-night stand murderer
Once again she plied her eye to tears of loneliness
But that man was not worth it and she stood with all her will

Her real love from the Halls of Hell, Mr Celibacy
declared: = I'm the man you want! And I want you too.
But I have been lately mad. I am a shootable mad bullock,
Jesus complex perhaps, celibate as the Great Almighty,
Nothing I like better than a half bottle of wine =
Now LouJac pops her head round the kitchen door
Finding the spineless stupid saviour – so-called – poet
muttering: I really have all the treasure I need now

That's the tribetale. Dear friend. Of the Queen of the Halls
of Hell. My name? Finnba Failure. I'm not saying the real one.
And your true biography my moon-kissed, iris-stroked friend?
I have told the recent vita, the Treasure of the Sierra Madre,
All my enemies want my oil-well derricks, the Bosch want my head.
None of you can have any of it. The whole treasure is for my
petlamb, dewdrops in her hair from the laurel leaves. Trim
haired the crown of laurel leaves upon her laureate's brow.

April 25 1999
From Apollinaire's
Le Trésor

Lou's the name on my lips

Wolves of every kind in the night
I know them inhuman beyond belief
The demon devil steals my heart
And he dumps it at his doorway
It's just a bairn's toy in his hands

Older wolves were more faithful to me
As are the smaller bowsie-wowsies
And the amorous soldiers in love with the babes
The women an elegant wonderful memory
In the same way as the wolves are sweet

But today times really are worst of all
The nightmare wolves are now tigers
And the infantry and the fascist Empires
The Caesars have turned into Vampires
Harshly cruel as our shell-rising Venus

Bye bye Rouveyre I'm leaving now
Climbing astride my giant horse
I am going soon heading for war
Without pure mercy & hawk-eyed severity
Just like the trench warriors of Epinal

Selling it off as a popular image
That Georgin was hyping in the forest
Where are they those beautiful soldiers
Soldiers lost dog-tags Where are the wars
Where are the blitzkreigs of yesterday

Oct 12 98
p79 Calligrames
C'est Lou qu'on la nommait